Low Fat Cookbook

————— ✦❧✦❧✦ —————

The Essential Low Fat Cookbook on All Day Clean Eating, Low Fat Recipes and Low Fat Diet Meals

Table of Contents

Introduction

D ue to our lifestyle we have started feeding our bodies with anything, without worrying how bad it can be. Yet we worry about how we look or keep checking the scales for losing extra flab and go for fad diets.

Low fat, low carbs, Gluten free, Dairy free, and Paleo diets are all the latest dietary revolutions in the modern cuisine and all these diets expect you to eat healthy food instead of going for bad food – pizza, burgers, soda etc and in some cases processed foods, grains and dairy as well which we crave for.

Whether it's starving ourselves or keeping a tab on calories, we add too much tension to our meals instead of just focusing on the healthy options available, flavors and colors that healthy food items can offer.

When you go for a diet option, choose an option which is well balanced. If you go for high protein diets instead of carbohydrates it can be bad for your health. Though high protein diets can help you lose weight faster, make you feel fuller and definitely burn more calories and are needed for strong body than carbohydrates but they put load on your kidneys and can also cause loss of calcium from bones.

Various high-protein diets claim that cutting carbs in favor of protein can help you to lose weight faster while still feeling satisfied. However, losing carbs from your diet completely can be detrimental to health. With diets there are several downsides, too much carbs can also increase the risk of diabetes and energy as they can disrupt the blood sugar levels. An ideal diet should be moderate in terms of the nutritional value it offers.

Proteins and carbohydrates and even good fats can help in shedding extra pounds and maintaining a good health. Go for lean meats, chicken, turkey, fish and complex carbohydrates like brown rice, brown bread etc and plenty of green veggies and fruits in your diet.

While you should eat healthy food on a regular basis, allow yourself some cheat days where you can gorge on yummy delicacies and alcohol. Whether you have a heart problem or any other ailment or you just want to stay fit and have healthy life.
While buying grocery for your food preparation, check the labels before buying and try to buy fresh food items instead of frozen foods. Keep a check-list of what you want to eat for a week and

buy your groceries accordingly. Try our low fat diets to maintain a healthy lifestyle.

Some tips to cut back on fat:

1. Choose mono and polyunsaturated fats to protect your heart. For example, instead of ghee or butter, try olive oil
2. Choose lean meat and remove the excess fat from the meat
3. Take small portions of food and divide your three meals into six or seven small meals.
4. Read food labels and buy healthy food items
5. Cut down junk food and replace with healthy food items like fruits and vegetables.
6. Try to cut back on carbs after 7 pm and eat proteins for breakfast to stay full for longer time.

The trademarks that are used are without any consent, and the publication of the trademark is without permission or backing by the trademark owner. All trademarks and brands within this book are for clarifying purposes only and are the owned by the owners themselves, not affiliated with this document.

Chapter 1:

Easy Breakfast Recipes

Try these healthy and nutritious breakfast recipes for a low calorie diet. Not only are they tasty but will also fit into your diet plans.

Healthy and delicious Oatmeal

What can beat utterly delicious and a complete breakfast than a energizing oatmeal to kick start your day!

Prep and Cook Time: 15 minutes

Calories: 366 kCal

Serves 2

Ingredients

- A cup of steel cut oats
- 1 cups water
- Honey or sugar for taste

- 1 cup almonds and raisins
- 1 cup milk

Directions:

1. Pour water in a saucepan and boil it.
2. Add oats to the saucepan and cook for about 5-10 mins. Stir the oats regularly so the oats don't clump together.
3. Now add almonds, raisins and honey, stir and cover the saucepan.
4. Turn off the heat and serve with milk.

Note: You can also add fruits to the oatmeal to make it tastier. If you cook oats with milk it will add approx. 150 calories to it depending on the milk type.

Easy to cook Frittata

Frittata is a simple and low calorie dish which can be served in lunch or dinner as well. In this recipe, we add zucchini and tomato which provide excellent nutrients.

Prep and Cooking Time: 30 minutes

Calories: 85 kCal

Serves: 4

Ingredients

- 2 eggs
- A pinch of turmeric
- ½ cup medium chopped onion
- 1 tbsp. chicken or vegetable
- 3 cloves of chopped garlic
- 2 cups sliced zucchini

- ½ cup of diced green chili
- 1 tomato and ½ cup cilantro
- Salt and pepper to taste
- Oil
- You can also add mushroom, potato, bell pepper broccoli, tofu or cauliflower

Directions

1. Pour oil in a skillet and add chopped onions and garlic. If you are adding chicken, cook the chicken first and remove it from the pan and add it later. Add other vegetables of your choice next starting with the veggies which take longer time to cook and then add the softer vegetables.

2. Add salt and any seasonings you want like oregano, paprika. Let the mixture cook for a minute and taste it. If needed, add more salt or seasoning

3. Spread the veggies evenly on the bottom of the pan.

4. Whisk the eggs and pour them over vegetables. Cook for some time until eggs begin to set.

5. Now you can put the pan in the oven and bake for 8-10 minutes at the temperature of 400°F until the eggs are set. If the eggs are set, you can pull the frittata from the oven.

6. Let it cool for five minutes and slice into wedges and serve.

Baked Kale Chips

Kale is the trending veggie and a low calorie low calorie nutritious snack. They are a good substitute for those fatty potato chips and great for snacking.

Prep and Cooking Time: 20 mins

Calories: 58 kCal

Serves 2

Ingredients

- Bunch of Kale
- Salt and pepper to taste
- 1 tbsp. olive oil

Directions

1. Clean the kale leaves thoroughly. Carefully remove the leaves from the stems and tear into small pieces.
2. Dry the kale leaves and sprinkle olive oil and salt on the leaves
3. Meanwhile preheat the oven to a temperature of 350.
4. Bake the kale leaves for approximately 15 minutes

Chapter 2:

Salads

Low fat salads are not just healthy, but trying it with some interesting ingredients can not only suit your taste buds but also make your diet much better and satisfying. Whether you try salads for breakfast, lunch or dinner, these recipes are healthy and delicious.

Kale Salad with Quinoa and Avocado
Prep and Cooking Time: 45 mins
Calories: 439 kCal
Serves 2

Ingredients
- 2/3 cup of quinoa
- 2/3 cup of water
- 1 bunch of torn kale

- 1/3 cup chopped red bell pepper
- 2 tbsp. green onion, chopped
- ½ cup diced avocado
- ¼ cup of olive oil
- 2 tbsp. lemon juice
- Cheese
- 1/3 cup diced olives
- Salt and pepper to taste

Directions:

1. Bring the water to a boil and add quinoa to the pan. Keep checkin quinoa in intervals until it becomes tender and the water is absorbed. Remove from pan and let it cool down.

2. Pour water in a saucepan and let it boil, add kale to it. Cover the pan with a lid and leave it like that for about a minute. Remove the kale from pan and let it cool down.

3. Once kale and quinoa cools down, add it on a large plate and top the kale with quinoa, bell pepper, green onion, olives and avocado.

4. Mix olive oil, lemon juice, salt and pepper together in a bowl and pour over the salad.

Summer Mediterranean Chickpea Salad

A diet rich in chickpea can lower your cholesterol levels. Reap the benefits of chickpea with this yummy salad

Prep and Cook Time: 40 minutes
Calories: 80 kCal

Serves 4

Ingredients

- 150g chickpeas, rinsed and drained
- 1 sliced onion
- 1 cucumber , peeled and chopped
- 3 chopped tomatoes
- 3 tomatoes, chopped
- 2 tbsp. olive oil
- Salt, pepper and oregano for taste
- 2-3 florets of broccoli
- 2 cloves garlic, chopped
- 3 tbsp. lemon juice

Directions:

1. Mix all the ingredients well in a large bowl.
2. Toss and mix it after adding lemon juice and olive oil
3. Let the flavors blend for some time and serve.

Fresh Lemon Greek Salad

Have this healthy recipe for lunch or dinner, bringing you the flavor of the beautiful Greek islands.

Prep and Cook Time: 10 minutes
Calories: 50 kCal
Serves 4

Ingredients

- 3 torn romaine/iceberg lettuce

- 1 torn escarole
- 1 thinly sliced red onions
- 1 sliced radish
- 1 tomato, sliced into 8 wedges
- 2 tbsp. lemon juice
- 2 tsp. olive oil
- 1 tbsp. yogurt
- 1 tsp. honey
- ½ tsp. dried oregano
- Salt and pepper for taste

Directions:

1. Combine the lettuce, escarole, radish, onion, tomato et al in a large bowl.
2. Mix it well with lemon juice, oil, yogurt, honey, and oregano in a jar, toss well.
3. Add salt and pepper to taste.
4. Pour over the salad and serve.
5.

Fresh and Filling Chef Salad with a twist

This recipe replaces the chef salad with blue cheese and rice cakes for a healthy version of a carb rich salad.

Prep and Cook Time: 10 minutes

Calories: 180 kCal
Serves 4

Ingredients

- ¼ cup of mayonnaise for salad dressing
- 2 tbsp. lemon juice
- ¼ tsp. black pepper
- 1 torn romaine lettuce
- 1 thinly sliced carrot
- 1 cup sliced and cooked chicken
- 1 chopped tomato
- 1 peeled and sliced cucumber
- 2 tbsp. crumbled blue cheese
- 2 brown rice cakes, crumbled

Directions:

1. Combine the veggies – lettuce, carrot, chicken, tomato and cucumber and blue cheese in a large bowl.
2. Add the salad dressings like lemon juice, salt and pepper in a measuring cup.
3. Toss it in a bowl and sprinkle with the brown rice cakes.
4. Shake it well and serve.

Chapter 3:

Eggs and more!

The omelet usually has eggs whisked together cooked with cheese or some veggies. Although adding cheese might not seem a great plan for your low fat diet but for all omelet lovers who are focusing on their diets, we have a few tricks up our sleeves to turn your omelet into a lean and healthy dish.

Berry omelet

Why have a plain omelet when you can mix it with up with fruits and make it a bit different.

Prep and Cook Time: 10 mins

Calories: 264 kCal

Serves 1

Ingredients

- 1 large egg
- 1 tbsp. skimmed milk
- 3 pinches of cinnamon
- 100g cottage cheese
- 150g chopped strawberries and blueberries
- Salt and pepper
- 1 tbsp. olive oil

Directions

1. Beat the egg and mix it with milk and cinnamon and add salt and pepper for taste and any seasonings if needed.
2. Pour oil in a nonstick frying pan and pour the egg mixture.
3. Cook for a few minutes until the egg is set.
4. Place the omelet on a plate and spread over cheese and cover it with strawberry and blueberry.

Mushroom and Basil Omelet with Tomato

Prep and Cook Time: 20 mins

Calories: 196 kCal

Serves 2

Ingredients

- 2 tomatoes

- 3 eggs
- 200g sliced mushrooms
- 1 teaspoon butter
- 2 tbsp. cheese
- 1 tbsp. finely chopped basil leaves

Directions

1. Break the eggs in a bowl and mix it well. Add a few drops of water, chives, salt and pepper and whisk the mixture well

2. Place tomatoes on a foil and put it in a grill. Heat it for some time until tomatoes are slightly burnt. Remove the tomatoes from the grill and squash them to release the juices.

3. Pour oil on a non-stick frying pan and add the mushrooms on pan. Let it cook for 5-10 minutes until mushrooms become tender. Remove it and set aside.

4. Now pour the egg mixture on the pan and top it with mushrooms, cheese, basil leaves and let it cook. Flip the other side of the omelet and leave it to cook.

5. Serve hot.

Chapter 4:

Low Fat Pasta

Mushroom pasta

Prep and Cook Time: 15-20 mins

Calories: 235

Serves: 2

Ingredients

- 250g mushrooms
- 250g penne or fusilli pasta
- Salt and paprika
- 3 cloves of sliced garlic
- Any vegetable like broccoli, capsicum, carrot, thinly sliced

Directions

1. Pour oil in a pan, add garlic and sauté it for a few minutes.

2. Now add vegetables of your choice and mushrooms in the pan and let it cook until the vegetables become soft.

3. Pour water and salt n another pan and let it boil.

4. In boiling water, add pasta and cook till it becomes a bit soft. Salt is added so the pasta doesn't stick together.

5. Drain the pasta and rinse with cold water.

6. Now toss pasta into the pan with vegetables. Mix well and let it cook.

7. Season with oregano and serve hot.

15 min pasta

Prep and Cook Time: 15 mins

Calories: 344

Serves 4

Easy and quick to get on the table than other objects and full of fresh veggies making it perfect for your diet.

Ingredients

- 400g pasta
- 1 chopped carrot and capsicum
- 1 chopped onion
- 5 medium tomatoes.
- 1 tsp. oregano
- Parmesan cheese
- Salt and red chili powder

Directions

1. Pour oil in a pan and add onions, sauté it for a few minutes until the onion turns transparents

2. Now add tomato and carrot in the pan and let it cook. Add salt and red chili powder. You can also blend garlic, tomato and onion to make a smooth paste.

3. Pour water and salt in another pan and let it boil.

4. In boiling water, add pasta and cook till it becomes a bit soft. Salt is added so the pasta doesn't stick together.

5. Drain the pasta and rinse with cold water.

6. Now toss pasta into the pan with vegetables. Mix well and let it cook.

7. Season with oregano and serve hot.

Light and tasty pasta with chicken and asparagus

Prep and Cooking Time: 30 mins

Calories: 330 kCal

Serves 2

Ingredients

- 1 /4 package of dried penne pasta
- 1 tbsp. olive oil
- ½ skinless, boneless chicken cut into halves
- Salt and pepper
- Garlic Power

- 2 tbsp. chicken broth
- ¼ bunch trimmed asparagus
- ¼ thinly sliced garlic cloves
- 1 tbsp. parmesan cheese

Directions

1. Pour water in a pan and add a little salt and let it boil
2. Once the water boils, add pasta and let it cook for approximately 10 minutes until pasta softens.
3. Drain the water and pour cold water on the pasta and set it aside.
4. Now add olive oil in a skillet and let it warm for some time.
5. Add chicken and salt, pepper, garlic powder and let it cook for approximately five minutes. Cook until the chicken softens and turns brown. Remove the chicken from the skillet and put in on a plate.
6. Now pour chicken broth on the skillet and add asparagus, garlic and a bit of salt or pepper if needed. Cover the skillet and let it cook until asparagus becomes tender for approximately 5-10 minutes.
7. T this mixture add chicken and pasta and mix well.
8. Let it sit for about 5 minutes and sprinkle olive oil and parmesan cheese
9. Serve hot

Chapter 5:

Low fat veg recipes

Healthy and veg rich Poha

Prep and Cook Time: 30 mins

Calories: 244 kCal

Serves 3

Ingredients

- 1.5 cups Poha - red or white beaten rice or flattened rice
- 1 chopped onion
- ¼ tsp. turmeric powder
- 1 tsp. mustard seeds
- 2 or 2.5 tbsp. peanuts
- 10-12 curry leaves
- 1 chopped green chili
- 1 chopped potato

- 1 thin sliced capsicum
- 1 thin sliced carrot
- 1 tsp. sugar or as required
- 1 or 1.5 tbsp. oil
- Salt

Directions

1. Firstly, rinse the Poha in water till they soften. You should be able to mash the Poha easily once they soften up.
2. Dry roast the peanuts in a pan till they become crunchy.
3. Heat oil in a pan and put onions in the pan and sauté till they turn translucent. Add salt, sugar, turmeric power, red chili powder and potato. Cook until the potato becomes soft.
4. Add curry leaves and green chilies in the pan and sauté for 2-3 minutes. Now add roasted peanuts, carrot, capsicum and stir. Check if all vegetables are cooked and if needed, add salt.
5. Add Poha in the mix and let it cook for 5-7 minutes on a medium flame.
6. Remove the lid and transfer the cooked Poha and sprinkle lemon juice, coriander leaves and grated coconut and bhujia.
7. Serve Poha hot with tea or with chutney.

Upma

Prep and Cook Time: 25 mins

Calories: 248 kCal

Serves 2

- 1 cup roasted semolina
- 1 chopped onion
- 1 chopped green chili
- 1 tbsp. chana dal/spilt and skinned Bengal gram
- ½ tbsp. urad dal/spilt and skinned
- ½ inch ginger grated or chopped finely
- 2.5 cups water
- 1 tsp. mustard seeds
- ½ tsp. cumin seeds
- 4-5 curry leaves
- 2 tbsp. olive oil
- Salt and red chili powder

Directions

1. Pour oil in a pan and let the oil heat up for some time and add mustard seeds. When they start giving a crackling sound, add cumin, chana dal and urad dal. Fry till this mix starts turning brown.
2. Add onion and sauté in this mix till it becomes transparent.
3. Add green chili, ginger, curry leaves and fry for a minute.
4. Pour water in the pan and let it boil, add roasted semolina and keep stirring so lumps don't get formed. Semolina can absorb water and it will swell once it's cooked. If it looks too dry, add some water and let it cook for 4-5 minutes.
5. Garnish Upma with coriander leaves and serve with green chutney or coconut chutney. You can also try Upma with sambhar.

Low calorie Nacho

This version of nachos has less calories than the traditional nachos, owing to baked tortilla chips, low fat beans and low fat cheese.

Prep and Cook Time: 15 minutes

Calories: 238 kCal

Serves 4

Ingredients

- ½ cup of chicken breast
- Baked tortilla chips
- ¼ cup of black beans
- 1 chopped tomato
- 4 tbsp. of low fat cheese

Directions:

1. Take a cookie sheet and place the chips and all the ingredients.
2. Place the tortilla chips on a cookie sheet and bake it for 5 minutes at 400°.
3. Serve hot.

Vegetarian Burritos

Veg Burritos are simple and delicious to pack for your lunch or your dinner. It can be prepared in as little as 20 minutes. We add spinach and mushroom to make it healthy and a bit of cheese to make it tasty.

Prep and Cook Time: 20 minutes

Calories: 229

Serves 1-2

Ingredients

- ½ cup chopped onion
- 2 cloves of chopped garlic
- 1 -2 fresh mushrooms
- A few spinach leaves
- Salt and pepper for taste
- 1 tbsp. lime juice
- ½ cup black beans
- Cheese
- 1 cup cooked brown rice
- Fresh salsa
- 8 (8-inch) whole-wheat flour tortilla

Directions

1. Pour olive oil over a skillet and add cumin seeds
2. Add onion, garlic and sauté it until the onions turn brown.
3. Next add jalapeno and mushrooms and sauté for 5 minutes. Add spinach leaves and let it cook for some time.
4. Add rice and beans and stir for 1-2 minutes
5. Add cheese until it melts.
6. On a non-stick pan, let the tortillas warm and spread the mixture on the tortilla and roll.
7. Serve hot with salsa if required.

Chapter 6:

Low fat chicken Dishes

Tandoori chicken

Prep and Cook Time: 45 mins

Calories: 171

Serves 2

Ingredients

- 2 sliced lemons
- 4 tsp. paprika
- 2 finely chopped onions
- 8 skinless chicken thigh pieces or breast pieces
- Olive oil

Preparation for the marinade

- 200 ml yogurt
- 1 grated ginger piece
- 2 cloves of finely chopped garlic
- ¾ tsp. garam masala
- ¾ tsp. ground cumin
- ½ tsp. chili powder
- ¼ tsp. turmeric

Directions

1. Blend onion, garlic and ginger along with garam masala, chili powder, paprika, turmeric in a mixer and pour this mixture into a large bowl.
2. Mix it with yogurt and place the chicken pieces in this bowl for approximately 60 mins.
3. Place the marinated chicken pieces in an oven and keep the temperature as 400 degrees. Splash a little oil over the pieces and let the chicken pieces grill on both sides until they are slightly charred and completely cooked.

Spicy yogurt chicken

Try a spicy twist with your chicken which works well hot or cold and is also a good source of iron.

Prep and Cook Time: 20-25 minutes

Calories: 180 kCal

Serves 4

Ingredients

- 8 pieces of boneless chicken breasts/thighs
- 150ml yogurt
- 1 tsp. chili powder
- 1 tbsp. ground cumin powder
- 1 tbsp. ground coriander
- 2 tsp. ground turmeric
- 1 tsp garam masala
- 2 cloves of finely chopped garlic
- 2 chopped onions

Method

1. Blend onion, garlic and ginger along with garam masala, chili powder, paprika, turmeric in a mixer and pour this mixture into a large bowl.
2. Mix it with yogurt and place the chicken pieces in this bowl for approximately 60 mins. Make sure to make a few cuts in the chicken pieces.
3. Heat the barbecue and cook the chicken pieces for a few minutes.
4. Cook for a few minutes until both sides are cooked.
5. Serve with mayonnaise or green chutney.

Chapter 7:

Low Fat Fish recipes

When it comes to a low fat diet, nothing can beat the taste of seafood. Whether it's cod, salmon – fish is a very smart option for your dinner or your lunch. It is rich in Omega-3 and reduces the risk of heart diseases. Fish can also absorb the flavor of any ingredients you try it whether citrus or spicy. We present some low fat recipes to let you have a fresh and delicious meal.

Classic Fish & Chips

Prep and Cook Time: 40 mins
Calories: 366
Serves: 4

Ingredients

- 3-4 potato, cut into chips
- 2 tbsp. olive oil
- 50g breadcrumbs
- 2 tbsp. chopped flat-leaf parsley
- 200g tomato
- 600g fish fillets
- 200g/ 7oz cherry tomato
- Lemon zest
- Parsley

Method

1. Heat oven to a temperature of 220C.
2. Let the potato chips dry and place on a baking tray. Sprinkle olive oil on the potato chips and season with salt. You need to cook the potato chips for 40 mins and ensure both sides are cooked evenly. So turn the potato to another side after 15-20 mins.
3. Mix the breadcrumbs with lemon zest and parsley. Add the fish fillets even in this breadcrumb mixture and splash some drops of olive oil.
4. Let this mixture bake with the tomatoes in oven for 10 mins and serve hot.

Roasted Cod

Prep and Cook Time: 45- 50 mins

Calories: 506 kCal

Serves: 4-6

Ingredients

- 3 thinly sliced lemons
- 8-9 medium potatoes
- 6 cod fillets
- Salt and pepper for taste
- 8 fresh thyme sprigs
- 10-15 green olives

Directions

1. Heat oven to a temperature of 450 degrees.
2. Place lemon slices in a layer on a baking pan and place thyme sprigs and olives
3. Cut the potatoes into half and place in a large bowl of water. Microwave it for 15 mins so that the potatoes are soft and can be easily pierced with a knife.
4. Drain the bowl and place the potatoes on the pan
5. Place fillets on the baking pan which contains the lemon slices.
6. Splash olive oil over cod and potatoes and season with salt and pepper
7. Place the pan in an oven and reduce temperatures to 325 degrees.
8. Roast the fish for about 25 minutes till the fish gets cooked thoroughly.
9. Garnish the dish with potatoes with olives and serve hot.

Chapter 8:

Smoothies and Shakes

Strawberry Smoothie

If you love smoothies, you will love this wonderful combination of taste and nutrition.

Prep and Cook Time: 5 minutes

Calories: 175 kCal

Serves 2

Ingredients

- 4 -5 strawberries
- ¼ cup plain yogurt
- 1 cup fresh orange juice
- 1 banana

Directions

10. Wash strawberries and remove it from the stem
11. Pour all the ingredients in a mixer and blend it.
12. Serve chilled.

Banana, Orange and Papaya Shake

This combo of orange, papaya and banana to make a filling drink that also keeps your cholesterol level low. This fruit drink will ensure you have an ample supply of nutrients like potassium, vitamin C and fiber. It will satiate your hunger and keep your skin glowing.

Prep and Cook Time: 5 minutes

Calories: 190

Serves 2

Ingredients

- 1 orange, separated into pieces
- ¼ sliced papaya
- 1 banana, cut into pieces
- Crushed ice

Directions

1. Put all the ingredients together with a little water.
2. Mix it well using a mixer or a blender
3. Strain the juice

4. Add crushed ice in glasses and serve immediately.

Apple Cinnamon Shake

Prep and Cook Time: 10 minutes

Calories: 145 kCal

Serves 4

Ingredients

- 3 chopped apples
- 1 cup soya milk
- 2 cups milk
- 1/2 tsp. cinnamon powder
- Sugar or honey
- Crushed ice

Directions

1. Blend the apple and sugar/honey in a mixer.
2. Add cinnamon powder and milk and blend again.
3. Add crushed ice in the glasses and pour the drink.
4. Serve immediately

Chapter 9:

Desserts

Yogurt with Fruit

A great recipe for a dessert or a breakfast

Prep and Cook Time: 15 minutes
Calories: 238 kCal
Serves 4

Ingredients
1 cup chopped apple
½ cup almonds and raisins
1 cup grapes
2 sliced bananas
½ cup pineapple
1 cup mango
Any seasonal fruit

2 cups yogurt

Directions
Mix all the fruit together in a bowl of yogurt and serve chilled.

Chocolate-Cherry Cookies

Prep and Cook Time: 40-50 minutes

Calories: 94 kCal

Serves: About 30 cookies

Ingredients

- 1/3 cup of all-purpose flour
- 1/3 cup of whole wheat flour
- 1.5 cups of rolled oats
- 1 tbsp. baking soda
- ½ tsp. salt
- 6 tbsp. butter
- ¾ cup brown sugar
- 1 cup dried cherries
- 1 tsp. vanilla extract
- 1 egg, slightly beaten
- 2 cups of dark chocolate, chopped

Directions
1. Weigh flours into measuring cups and combine the flour, oats, baking soda and salt in a large bowl and stir well.

2. Melt butter in a small saucepan over low heat and add brown sugar. Stir until the mixture becomes smooth

3. Combine the sugar and flour mixture and blend it in a mixer.

4. Add cherry, vanilla extract, egg and beat well.

5. Add chocolate and drop this mix into baking sheets.

6. Now add the baking sheet in the oven and keep the temperature of oven to 350°.

7. Let it cool down and serve.

8. You can also refrigerate it and serve it when required.

Conclusion

Fitness is one of the most critical things for achieving good health. It does not mean that you have to become a fitness freak. You should start by setting achievable and motivating targets- like working out for three to four days a week or taking the stairs instead of lift or walking to your office instead of taking your car.

Begin with small changes and then incorporate more exercises into your schedule. You can try swimming, playing sports, cycling or kickboxing, power yoga. Make your workouts enjoyable by joining dance, aerobics or zumba classes. Regular exercises would increase your heart rate, improve blood circulation and release excess toxins by constant sweating.

There is no dearth of options, all you have to do is take the first step to be on the road to fitness. Try to find something you enjoy and do it regularly, these exercises will keep your heart active and blood pumping! Enjoy!

Made in the USA
Middletown, DE
08 May 2022

65477256R00029